WRITINGS TO YOUNG WOMEN FROM

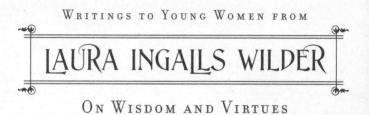

LAURA INGALLS WILDER

ON WISDOM AND VIRTUES

VOLUME ONE

Laura Ingalls Wilder

Edited by Stephen W. Hines

TOMMY NELSON™
FOR TWEENS AND TEENS

A Division of Thomas Nelson Publishers
Since 1798

www.thomasnelson.com

Writings to Young Women from Laura Ingalls Wilder:
On Wisdom and Virtues
Volume One
Adapted from *Little House in the Ozarks*

Published in Nashville, Tennessee, by Tommy Nelson®, a Division of Thomas Nelson, Inc. Visit us on the Web at www.tommynelson.com.

Tommy Nelson® books may be purchased in bulk for educational, business, fund-raising, or sales promotional use. For information, please e-mail:
SpecialMarkets@ThomasNelson.com.

Scripture quotations are from *The Holy Bible, King James Version*.

This book is not in any way sponsored by or affiliated with HarperCollins Publishers, which claims the exclusive right to use the words "Little House" as a trademark. Our use of these words simply and truthfully brings to you the warm personal facts about Laura Ingalls Wilder, America's beloved author, and about her life, times, and beliefs.

Cover photograph credits: Laura at seventeen (center), Laura's writing desk (*Mansfield Mirror*, Courtesy of State Historical Society of Missouri), Laura's profile (Herbert Hoover Presidential Library), "For Those Who Sew" advertisement (The Kansas State Historical Society), Laura (The Kansas State Historical Society), "You Can Make Your Own Hat" advertisement (The Kansas State Historical Society).

Library of Congress Cataloging-in-Publication Data

Wilder, Laura Ingalls, 1867-1957.
  [Prose works. Selections]
  Writings to young women from Laura Ingalls Wilder / Laura Ingalls Wilder ; edited by Stephen W. Hines.
    p. cm.
  ISBN 1-4003-0784-8 (*On Wisdom and Virtues*, Volume One)
  1. Young women—Conduct of life. I. Hines, Stephen W. II. Title.
PS3545.I342A6 2006
814'.52—dc22

2005033723

Printed in the United States of America

06 07 08 09 10 WRZ 9 8 7 6 5 4 3 2 1

WRITINGS TO YOUNG WOMEN FROM

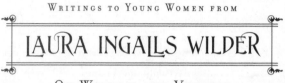

LAURA INGALLS WILDER

ON WISDOM AND VIRTUES

VOLUME ONE

CONTENTS

FOREWORD

Laura Ingalls Wilder was born in the nineteenth century in the year 1867. She grew up, married, and lived out most of her life during the era of the western pioneers. Her father, Charles "Pa" Ingalls, was definitely an early pioneer, having moved west with his own family from Cuba, New York, around the year 1850. Laura herself was born early enough in the history of our country to have heard Native Americans dancing and chanting not far from her farm cabin in Kansas.

All of this is written about in eight books that came to be the basis for *The Little House on the Prairie* TV program that can still be seen in reruns on cable TV. Laura's life was so typical of what it was like during pioneering days that even in this century, Walt Disney Studios made a five-part series about her life on the prairie.

What most people don't know about Laura is that after becoming an adult, she was among the first of a group of women to practice the profession of journalism, writing as a columnist and reporter for many years. She was extremely proud of her career and of her writing. She kept a scrapbook, which contained the first piece she ever wrote to the newspapers, a short letter dating from the 1890s.

Laura's professional career didn't begin until she was in her forties and her own daughter was working as a reporter in California. *The Missouri Ruralist*, which still publishes today, gave Laura her entrance into journalism and promoted her work for some fifteen years, until she began working on her classic stories of her family and pioneer life.

"Ma"—Caroline Lake Quinter Ingalls

South Dakota State Historical Society

"Pa"—Charles Philip Ingalls

South Dakota State Historical Society

The founding family of the town of De Smet, South Dakota. Ma and Pa Ingalls and the girls—from left to right—Caroline Lake Quinter Ingalls, Caroline (Carrie) Celestia Ingalls, Laura Elizabeth Ingalls, Charles Philip Ingalls, Grace Pearl Ingalls, and Mary Amelia Ingalls.

By that time, Laura was in her sixties, but she continued to learn and try new things; so when others were retiring from work, she was launching yet a new career as a book author! Today, her books can be found in bookstores and libraries all over the country.

Although Laura Ingalls Wilder's fame is worldwide, with over ten million copies of her books sold, the writings gathered in this book from her journalistic period are treasures, too. *The Missouri Ruralist* was right to single out Mrs. Wilder for attention, because she wrote of timeless things people of any age can relate to.

You will see in *Writings to Young Women from Laura Ingalls Wilder: On Wisdom and Virtues* that nothing of real importance ever changes. Her concerns are not so different from the ones we have today, though they take different form. These columns and anecdotes show Laura struggling with worry, purpose, and the meaning of life.

Mrs. Wilder meditates on the fact that even her little dog, Incubus, who is blind, must sometimes wonder about why such things happen in this life. Then Incubus decides in his own doggy way to get on with living as best he can, and Laura feeds him.

Laura is also concerned that we make good choices in life, and she lays down principles that are still good for us to consider. Are we overworked? Perhaps we should plan better or put aside some of the hustle and bustle for another day. Do we sometimes hurt the feelings of our friends? Laura would have us pause to consider the words of a poet. Do we sometimes slip and take the name of the Lord in vain? Laura would have us realize that this is always wrong, no matter the reason for it.

In "Do the Right Thing Always," Mrs. Wilder writes: "If there were a cry of 'stop, thief!' we would all stand still. Yet nevertheless, in spite of our carelessness, we all know deep in our hearts that it pays to do the right thing, though it is easy to deceive ourselves for a time. If we do the wrong thing, we are quite likely never to know what we have lost by it."

Fortunately, we do not have to learn all our lessons the hard way if we trust in the guidance of someone who has gone on before us like Laura.

Stephen W. Hines
Editor

ACKNOWLEDGMENTS

First of all, I would like to acknowledge the invaluable aid of my wife, Gwendolyn Joy Hines, in this undertaking. Her persistence in proofreading, titling of articles, and all-around general good advice made this project flow much more smoothly than it would have otherwise.

And my thanks to:

Gordon R. Cuany for obtaining material for me through interlibrary loan.

Jackie Dana for her determined research efforts at the Ellis Library of the University of Missouri at Columbia, Missouri.

Patricia Timberlake, June DeWeese, Margaret Howell, Laurel Boeckman, Marie Concannon, librarians at the Ellis Library, who answered my questions and allowed me to review highly fragile material.

Suzanne Lippard, library clerk, for her fund of personal

information about Laura Ingalls Wilder and about the people still living who had known her.

Marion Bond, library assistant for the Kansas State Historical Society, for invaluable help in speeding my research.

Dwight Miller, now retired, who as head of the Herbert Hoover Library in West Branch, Iowa, helped me track down archival material.

Bruce Barbour, former publisher of Thomas Nelson Trade Books, for backing the lengthy efforts of *Little House in the Ozarks*, from which this current project was adapted.

Bill Watkins, former Senior Editor at Thomas Nelson Trade Books, for his alert eye in going over the manuscript for *Little House in the Ozarks*.

And special thanks to Jennifer Gingerich, Backlist Editor for Tommy Nelson, for making this current project possible.

ONE

IT PAYS TO DO THE RIGHT THING

*"Is it possible that 'honesty is the best policy,'
after all, actually and literally?"*

The Helping Hand of Helpfulness

I know a little band of friends that calls itself a woman's club. The avowed purpose of this club is study, but there is an undercurrent of deeper, truer things than even culture and self-improvement. There is no obligation, and there are no promises; but in forming the club and in selecting new members, only those are chosen who are kindhearted and dependable as well as the possessors of a certain degree of intelligence and a small amount of that genius which is the capacity for careful work. In short, those who are taken into membership are those who will make good friends, and so they are a little band who are each for all and all for each.

If one needs the helping hand of comradeship, not one but all are eager and willing to help, with financial aid if needed, but more often with a good word or a small act of kindness. They are getting so in the habit of speaking good words that I expect to see them all develop into Golden Gossips.

> Cooperation, helpfulness, and fair dealing are so badly needed in the world, and if they are not learned as children at home, it is difficult for grownups to have a working knowledge of them.

Ever hear of golden gossip? I read of it some years ago. A woman who was always talking about her friends and neighbors made it her business to talk of them, in fact, never said anything but good of them. She was a gossip, but it was "golden gossip." This woman's club seems to be working in the same way and associations of friendship and mutual helpfulness are being built up which will last for life. It is a beautiful thing, and more than ever one is impressed with the idea that it is a pity there are—

> *So many gods, so many creeds,*
> *So many paths that wind and wind*

When just the art of being kind
Is all the sad world needs. *

❧

"Money is the root of all evil," says the proverb, but I think that proverb maker only dug down part way around the plant of evil. If he had really gotten to the root of the matter, I am sure he would have found that root to be selfishness—just selfishness pure and simple. Why all the mad scramble for money? Why are we all "money-mad Americans"? It is just for our selfish gratification with things that money can buy, from world dominion to a stick of striped candy—selfishness, just selfishness.

Not long ago, I was visiting in a family where there were several children. The father lost his memorandum book and was inquiring for it. No one had seen it. "I wish," he said, "that you children would find it for me before I come back at noon." There was silence for a minute, and then one of the children said: "Why don't you put up a quarter? That'll find it!"

"Well, I will," his father answered, and at once the children were all eagerness to search. It seemed to me such a pity to appeal to a selfish interest in the home where there should be loving service freely given.

---

* From "The World's Need," by Ella Wheeler Wilcox

In the blacksmith shop, one hot day last summer, the blacksmith was sweating over his hot irons when two idle boys sauntered in and over to the water bucket. It was empty. "Ain't yuh got no water?" asked one of the boys.

"Not if the bucket is empty," answered the blacksmith.

Then the man for whom the blacksmith was working spoke up. "Why don't you go get a bucket of water?" he asked.

"I will for a nickel," said the boy.

"Yes, we'll go for a nickel," agreed the other boy.

"Were you going to pay for your drink?" asked the man innocently, and the boys looked at him surprised and then slunk away without filling the bucket. Just an example of selfishness made more contemptible by being so plainly unfair.

Cooperation, helpfulness, and fair dealing are so badly needed in the world, and if they are not learned as children at home, it is difficult for grownups to have a working knowledge of them.

So much depends on starting the children right!

Let Us Be Just
SEPTEMBER 1917

Two little girls had disagreed, as was to be expected, because they were so temperamentally different. They wanted to play in different ways, and as they had to play together, all operations were stopped while they argued the question. The elder of the two had a sharp tongue and great facility in using it. The other was slow to speak but quick to act, and they both did their best according to their abilities.

> I hate to write the end of the story. No, not the end! No story is ever ended!

Said the first little girl: "You've got a snub nose and your hair is just a common brown color. I heard Aunt Lottie say so! Ah, don't you wish your hair was a b-e-a-u-tiful golden like mine, and your nose a fine shape? Cousin Louisa said that about me. I heard her!"

The second little girl could not deny these things. Her dark skin, brown hair, and snub nose, as compared with her sister's lighter coloring and regular features, were a tragedy in her little life. She could think of nothing cutting to reply, for she was not given to saying unkind things nor was her tongue nimble enough to say them, so she stood digging her bare toes into the ground, hurt, helpless, and tongue-tied.

The first girl, seeing the effect of her words, talked on. "Besides, you're two years younger than I am, and I know more than you, so you have to mind me and do as I say!"

This was too much! Sister was prettier, no answer

could be made to that. She was older, it could not be denied; but that gave her no right to command. At last here was a chance to act!

Mrs. Laura Ingalls Wilder at the height of her writing career

"And you have to mind me," repeated the first little girl.

"I will not!" said the second little girl, and then, to show her utter contempt for such authority, this little brown girl slapped her elder, golden-haired sister.

I hate to write the end of the story. No, not the end! No story is ever ended! It goes on, and on, and the effects of this one followed this little girl all her life, showing her hatred of injustice. I should say that I dislike to tell what came next, for the golden-haired sister ran crying and told what had happened, except her own part in the quarrel, and the little brown girl was severely punished. To be plain, she was soundly spanked and set in a corner.

> It was not the pain of the punishment that hurt so much as the sense of injustice.

She did not cry but sat glowering at the parent who punished her and thinking in her rebellious little mind that when she was large enough, she would return the spanking with interest.

It was not the pain of the punishment that hurt so much as the sense of injustice, the knowledge that she had not been treated fairly by one from whom she had the right to expect fair treatment, and that there had been a failure to understand where she had thought a mistake impossible. She had been beaten and bruised by sister's unkind words and had been unable to reply. She had defended herself in the only way possible for her and felt that she had a perfect right to do so, or if not, then both should have been punished.

Children have a fine sense of justice that sometimes is far truer than that of older persons, and in almost every case, if appealed to, will prove the best help in governing them. When children are ruled through their sense of justice, there are no angry thoughts left to rankle in their minds. Then a punishment is not an injury inflicted upon them by someone who is larger and stronger but the inevitable consequence of their own acts, and a child's mind will understand this much sooner than one would think. What a help all their lives in self-control and self-government this kind of a training would be!

We are prone to put so much emphasis on the desirability of mercy that we overlook the beauties of the principle of justice. The quality of mercy is a gracious, beautiful thing; but with more justice in the world, there would be less need for mercy, and exact justice is most merciful in the end.

The difficulty is that we are so likely to make mistakes, we cannot trust our judgment and so must be merciful to offset our own shortcomings; but I feel sure when we are able to comprehend the workings of the principle of justice, we shall find that instead of being opposed to each other, infallible justice and mercy are one and the same thing.

If We Only Understood
DECEMBER 1917

Mrs. Brown was queer. The neighbors all thought so and, what was worse, they said so.

Mrs. Fuller happened in several times, quite early in the morning, and although the work was not done up, Mrs. Brown was sitting leisurely in her room or else she would be writing at her desk. Then Mrs. Powers went through the house one afternoon, and the dishes were stacked back unwashed, the bed still airing, and everything "at sixes and sevens," except the room where Mrs. Brown seemed to be idling away her time. Mrs. Powers said Mrs. Brown was "just plain lazy," and she didn't care who heard her say it.

Ida Brown added interesting information when she told her schoolmates, after school, that she must hurry home and do up the work. It

> The safest course is to be as understanding as possible, and, where our understanding fails, to call charity to its aid.

was a shame, the neighbors said, that Mrs. Brown should idle away her time all day and leave the work for Ida to do after school.

Later, it was learned that Mrs. Brown had been writing for the papers to earn money to buy Ida's new winter outfit. Ida had been glad to help by doing the work after school so that her mother might have the day for study and writing, but they had not thought it necessary to explain to the neighbors.

I read a little verse a few years ago entitled, "If We Only Understood," and the refrain was:

> *We would love each other better,*
> *If we only understood.*

I have forgotten the author and last verse, but the refrain has remained in my memory and comes to my mind every now and then when I hear unkind remarks made about people.

The things that people do would look so differently to us if we only understood the reasons for their actions, nor would we blame them so much for their faults if we knew all the circumstances of their lives. Even their sins might not look so hideous if we could feel what pressure and perhaps suffering had caused them.

The safest course is to be as understanding as possible, and, where our understanding fails, to call charity to its aid. Learn to distinguish between persons and the things they do, and while we may not always approve of their actions, have a sympathy and feeling of kindness for the persons themselves.

It may even be that what we consider faults and weaknesses in others are only prejudices on our own part. Some of us would like to see everybody fitted to our own pattern, and what a tiresome world this would be if that were done. We should be willing to allow others the freedom we demand for ourselves. Everyone has the right to self-expression.

If we keep this genial attitude toward the world and the people in it, we will keep our own minds and feelings healthy and clean. Even the vigilance necessary to guard our thoughts in this way will bring us rewards in better disciplined minds and happier dispositions.

A Dog's a Dog for A' That
AUGUST 1916

A redbird swinging in the grape arbor saw himself in the glass of my kitchen window not long ago. He tried to fly through the glass to reach the strange bird he saw there, and when his little mate came flitting by, he tried to fight his reflection. Apparently, he was jealous. During all one day, he fretted and struggled to drive the stranger away. He must have told his little wife about it that night, I think, for in the morning they came to the arbor together, and she alighted before the window while he stayed in the background. She gave Mr. Redbird one look after glancing in the glass, then turned and flew fiercely at her reflection, twittering angrily. One could imagine her saying: "So, that's it! This strange lady Redbird is the reason for your hanging around here instead of getting busy building the nest. I'll soon drive her away!" She tried to fight the strange lady bird until her husband objected to her paying so much attention to her rival; and then they took turns, he declaring there was a gentleman there, she vowing there was a lady and doing her best to drive her away. At last between them, they seemed to understand; and now they both come occasionally to swing on the grapevine before the window and admire themselves in the glass.

> There are many interesting things in the out-of-doors life that come so close to us in the country, and if we show a little kindness to the wild creatures, they quickly make friends with us.

There are many interesting things in the out-of-doors life that come so close to us in the country, and if we show a little kindness to the wild creatures, they quickly make friends with us and permit us a delightful intimacy with them and their homes. A bird in a cage is not a pretty sight to me, but it is a pleasure to have the wild birds and the squirrels nesting around the house and so tame that they do not mind our watching them. Persons who shoot or allow shooting on their farms drive away a great deal of amusement and pleasure with the game, as well as do themselves pecuniary damage, while a small boy with a stone handy can do even more mischief than a man with a gun.

It is surprising how like human beings animals seem when they are treated with consideration. Did you ever notice the sense of humor animals have? Ever see a dog apologize—not a cringing fawning for favor, but a frank apology as one gentleman to another?

> It is surprising how like human beings animals seem when they are treated with consideration.

Shep was trying to learn to sit up and shake hands, but try as he would, he could not seem to get the knack of keeping his balance in the upright position. He was an old dog, and you know it has been said that "It is hard to teach an old dog new tricks." No sympathy has ever been wasted on the dog, but I can assure you that it also is hard for the old dog. After a particularly disheartening session one day, we saw him out on the back porch alone and not knowing that he was observed. He was practicing his lesson without a teacher. We watched while he tried and failed several times, then finally got the trick of it and sat up with his paw extended. The next time we said, "How do you do, Shep?"

he had his lesson perfectly. After that it was easy to teach him to fold his paws and be a "Teddy Bear" and to tell us what he said to tramps. We never asked him to lie down and roll over. He was not that kind of character. Shep never would do his tricks for anyone but us, though he would shake hands with others when we told him to do so. His eyesight became poor as he grew older, and he did not always recognize his friends. Once he made a mistake and barked savagely at an old friend whom he really regarded as one of the family, though he had not seen him for some time.

> I feel that in his little doggy heart, he is asking the eternal "Why?" as we all do at times.

Later, as we all sat in the yard, Shep seemed uneasy. Evidently, there was something on his mind. At last he walked deliberately to the visitor, sat up, and held out his paw. It was so plainly an apology that our friend said: "That's all right, Shep, old fellow! Shake and forget it!" Shep shook hands and walked away perfectly satisfied.

My little French poodle, Incubus, is blind. He used to be very active and run about the farm, but his chief duty, as he saw it, was to protect me. Although he cannot see, he still performs that duty, guarding me at night and flying at any stranger who comes too near me during the day. Of what he is thinking when he sits for long periods in the yard with his face to the sun, I am too stupid to understand perfectly, but I feel that in his little doggy heart, he is asking the eternal "Why?" as we all do at times. After a while he seemingly decides to make the best of it and takes a walk around the familiar places or comes in the house and does his little tricks for candy with a cheery good will.

If patience and cheerfulness and courage, if being faithful to our trust and doing our duty under difficulties count for so much in man that he expects to be rewarded for them, both here and hereafter, how are they any less in the life of my little blind dog? Surely, such virtues in animals are worth counting in the sum total of good in the universe.

A Few Minutes with a Poet
JANUARY 1919

Among my books of verse, there is an old poem that I could scarcely do without. It is "The Fool's Prayer" by Edward Rowland Sill, and every now and then I have been impelled in deep humiliation of spirit to pray the prayer made by that old-time jester of the king. Even though one is not in the habit of making New Year's resolutions, to be broken whenever the opportunity arises, still, as the old year departs, like Lot's wife, we cannot resist a backward glance. As we see in retrospect, the things we have done that we ought not and the things we have left undone that we should have done, we have a hope that the coming year will show a better record.

In my glance backward and hope for the future, one thing became plain to me—that I valued the love and appreciation of my friends more than ever before, and that I would try to show my love for them; that I would be more careful of their feelings, more tactful, and so endear myself to them.

> To laugh and forget is one of the saving graces.

A few days later a friend and I went together to an afternoon gathering where refreshments were served, and we came back to my friend's home just as the evening meal was ready. The Man of the Place failed to meet me, and so I stayed unexpectedly. My friend made apologies for the simple meal, and I said that I preferred plain food to such as we had in the afternoon, which was the same as saying that her meal was plain and that the afternoon refreshments had been finer. I felt that I had said the wrong thing, and in a desperate effort to make amends, I praised the soup which had been served. Not being satisfied to let well enough alone, because of my embarrassment I continued, "It is so easy to have delicious soups, one can make them of just any little things that are left." And all the way home as I rode quietly beside the Man of the Place, I kept praying "The Fool's Prayer": "O LORD, be merciful to me, a fool."

> Our hearts are mostly in the right place, but we seem weak in the head.

We can afford to laugh at a little mistake such as that, however embarrassing it may be. To laugh and forget is one of the saving graces, but only a little later I was guilty of another mistake over which I could not laugh. Mrs. G and I were in a group of women at a social affair; but having a little business to talk over, we stepped into another room where we were almost immediately followed by an acquaintance. We greeted her and then went on with our conversation, from which she was excluded. I forgot her presence, and then I looked her way again; she was gone. We had not been kind, and to make it worse, she was comparatively a stranger among us.

In a few minutes everyone was leaving without my having had a chance to make amends in any way. I could not apologize without giving a point to the rudeness, but I thought that I would be especially gracious to her when we met again so she would not feel that we made her an outsider. Now I learn that it will be months before I see her again. I know that she is very sensitive and that I must have hurt her. Again and from the bottom of my heart, I prayed "The Fool's Prayer":

> *These clumsy feet, still in the mire,*
> *Go crushing blossoms without end;*
> *These hard, well-meaning hands we thrust*
> *Among the heart-strings of a friend—*
> *O LORD, be merciful to me, a fool.*

As we grow old enough to have a proper perspective, we see such things work out to their conclusion or rather to a partial conclusion, for the effects go on and on endlessly. Very few of our misdeeds are with deliberate intent to do wrong. Our hearts are mostly in the right place, but we seem to be weak in the head.

> *'Tis not by guilt the onward sweep*
> *Of truth and right, O LORD, we stay;*
> *'Tis by our follies that so long*
> *We hold the earth from heaven away.*
> *Our faults no tenderness should ask;*
> *The Chastening stripes must cleanse them all;*
> *But for our blunder—oh, in shame*
> *Before the eyes of heaven we fall.*

Without doubt each one of us is fully entitled to pray the whole of "The Fool's Prayer" and more especially the refrain: "O Lord, be merciful to me, a fool."

Do the Right Thing Always
JUNE 1918

It is always best to treat people right," remarked my lawyer friend.

"Yes, I suppose so in the end," I replied inanely.

"Oh, of course!" he returned, "but that was not what I meant. It pays every time to do the right thing! It pays now and in dollars and cents."

"For instance?" I asked.

"Well, for the latest instance: a man came to me the other day to bring suit against a neighbor. He had good grounds for damages and could win the suit, but it would cost him more than he could recover. It would increase his neighbor's expenses and increase the bad feeling between them. I needed that attorney's fee; but it would not have been doing the right thing to encourage him to bring suit, so I advised him to settle out of court. He insisted, but I refused to take

> Is it possible that "honesty is the best policy," after all, actually and literally?

the case. He hired another lawyer, won his case, and paid the difference between the damages he recovered and his expenses.

"A client came to me a short time afterward with a worthwhile suit and a good retainer's fee, which I could take without robbing him. He was sent to me by the man whose case I had refused to take and because of that very refusal."

> To do the right thing is simply to be honest.

Is it possible that "honesty is the best policy," after all, actually and literally? I would take the advice of my lawyer friend on any other business, and I have his word for it that it pays to do the right thing here and now.

To do the right thing is simply to be honest, for being honest is more than refraining from shortchanging a customer or robbing a neighbor's hen roost. To be sure, those items are included, but there is more to honesty than that. There is such a thing as being dishonest when no question of financial gain or loss is involved. When one person robs another of his good name, he is dishonest. When by an unnecessary, unkind act or cross word, one causes another to lose a day or an hour of happiness, is that one not a thief? Many a person robs another of the joy of life while taking pride in his own integrity.

We steal from today to give to tomorrow; we "rob

Peter to pay Paul." We are not honest even with ourselves; we rob ourselves of health; we cheat ourselves with sophistries; we even "put an enemy in our mouths to steal away our brains."

If there were a cry of "Stop thief!" we would all stand still. Yet nevertheless in spite of our carelessness, we all know deep in our hearts that it pays to do the right thing, though it is easy to deceive ourselves for a time. If we do the wrong thing, we are quite likely never to know what we have lost by it. If the lawyer

> If there were a cry of "Stop thief!" we would all stand still.

had taken the first case, he might have thought he gained by so doing, for he never would have known of the larger fee which came to him by taking the other course.

Kind Hearts
MARCH 1922

Officially, winter is over and spring is here. For most of us, it has been a hard winter despite the fact that the weather has been pleasant the greater part of the time. There are things other than zero weather and heavy snowfalls that make hard winters.

But we know all about those things, and so I'll tell you

of something else—something as warming to the heart as a good fire on the hearth is to a chilled body on a cold day.

I often have thought that we are a little old-fashioned here in the Ozark hills; now I know we are, because we had a "working" in our neighborhood this winter. That is a blessed, old-fashioned way of helping out a neighbor.

While the winter was warm, still it has been much too cold to be without firewood; and this neighbor, badly crippled with rheumatism, was not able to get up his winter's wood. With what little wood he could manage to chop, the family scarcely kept comfortable.

So the men of the neighborhood gathered together one morning and dropped in on him. With cross-cut saws and axes, they took possession of his wood lot. At noon a wood saw was brought in, and it sawed briskly all the afternoon. By night there was enough wood ready for the stove to last the rest of the winter.

> I often have thought that we are a little old-fashioned here in the Ozark hills; now I know we are.

The women did their part, too. All morning they kept arriving with well-filled baskets, and at noon a long table was filled with a country neighborhood dinner.

After the hungry men had eaten and gone back to work, the women and children gathered at the second table, fully as well supplied as the first, and chatted pleasant neighborhood gossip while they leisurely enjoyed the good things. Then when the dishes were washed, they sewed, knit, and crocheted and talked for the rest of the afternoon.

It was a regular old-fashioned good time, and we all went home with the feeling expressed by a newcomer when he said, "Don't you know I'm proud to live in a neighborhood like this where they turn out and help one another when it's needed."

"Sweet are the uses of adversity" when it shows us the kindness in our neighbors' hearts.

Everyday Implications of the Golden Rule
MAY 1922

Some small boys went into my neighbor's yard this spring and with slingshots killed the wild birds that were nesting there. Only the other day, I read in my daily paper of several murders committed by a nineteen-year-old boy.

At once there was formed a connection in my mind between the two crimes, for both were crimes of the same kind, though perhaps in differing degree—the breaking of laws and the taking of life cruelly.

For the cruel child to become a hard-hearted boy and then a brutal man is only stepping along the road on which he has started. A child allowed to disobey without punishment is not likely to have much respect for law as he grows older—not that every child who kills birds becomes a murderer, nor that everyone who is not taught to obey goes to prison.

The Bible says, "Train up a child in the way he should go and when he is old, he will not depart from it."* The opposite is also true, and if a child is started in the way he should not go, he will go at least some way along that road as he grows older. It will always be more difficult for him to travel the right way even though he finds it.

> I am sure we will all agree that these laws of ours should be as wise and as few as possible.

The first laws with which children come in contact are the commands of their parents. Few fathers and mothers are wise in giving these, for we are all so busy and thoughtless. But I am sure we will all agree that these laws of ours should be as wise and as few as possible, and, once given, children should be made to obey or shown that to disobey brings punishment. Thus they will learn the lesson every good citizen and every good man and woman learns sooner or later—that breaking a law brings suffering.

---

* Proverbs 22:6

If we break a law of nature, we are punished physically; when we disobey God's law we suffer spiritually, mentally, and usually in our bodies also; man's laws, being founded on the Ten Commandments, are really mankind's poor attempt at interpreting the laws of God, and for disobeying them there is a penalty. The commands we give our children should be our translation of these laws of God and man, founded on justice and the law of love, which is the Golden Rule.

And these things enter into such small deeds. Even insisting that children pick up and put away their playthings is teaching them order, the law of the universe, and helpfulness, the expression of love.

The responsibility for starting the child in the right way is the parents'—it cannot be delegated to the schools or to the state, for the little feet start on life's journey from the home.

TWO

HOW MUCH ARE YOUR WORDS WORTH?

"If we want vegetables, we must make them grow, not leave the ground barren where we have destroyed the weeds."

A Man's Word Is All He Has
SEPTEMBER 1922

It is said that "money is the root of all evil," but money that is at the root of any evil in itself represents selfishness. . . .

It would be nearer the truth to say that selfishness is the root of evil and the overvaluation of money only one manifestation of it.

Money hasn't any value of its own; it represents the stored-up energy of men and women and is really just someone's promise to pay a certain amount of that energy.

It is the promise that has the real value. If no dependence can be put on the promises of a nation, then the currency of that nation, which is its promise to pay, is worthless. Bank notes depend for their value on the credit of the bank that issues them, and a man's note is good or not according to whether his promise to pay can be relied on.

> If there were only one thing of any value in this world and it were in our possession, how precious it would be to us.

So it comes to this: that as the business of the world is done on credit, a man's word, backed by his character, is the unit of value; and that character is the root of good or evil, making his word good or worthless.

If there were only one thing of any value in this world and it were in our possession, how precious it would be to us. How carefully we would guard it from all smirching or damaging, defending it with our lives if necessary! There would be no carelessness in the keeping of it, no reckless giving of it here and there as though it amounted to nothing.

Listen then to this Eastern proverb: "In this world, a man's word is all he has that is of real value; it is at the bottom of all other values."

Just a Question of Tact
OCTOBER 1916

You have so much tact and can get along with people so well," said a friend to me once. Then, after a thoughtful pause, she added, "But I never could see any difference between tact and trickery." Upon my assuring her that there was no difference, she pursued the subject further.

"Now I have no tact whatever, but speak plainly," she said pridefully. "The Scotch people are, I think, the most tactful, and the Scotch, you know, are the trickiest nation in the world."

As I am of Scotch descent, I could restrain my merriment no longer, and when I recovered enough to say, "You are right, I am Scotch," she smiled ruefully and said, "I told you I had no tact."

Tact does for life just what lubricating oil does for machinery. It makes the wheels run smoothly, and without it there is a great deal of friction and the possibility of a breakdown. Many a car on the way of life fails to make the trip as expected for lack of this lubricant.

> "I told you I had no tact."

Tact is a quality that may be acquired. It is only the other way of seeing and presenting a subject. There are always two sides to a thing, you know; and if one side is disagreeable, the reverse is quite apt to be very pleasant. The tactful person may see both sides but uses the pleasant one.

"Your teeth are so pretty when you keep them white," said Ida to Stella, which, of course, was equal to saying that Stella's teeth were ugly when she did not keep them clean, as frequently happened; but Stella left her friend with the feeling that she had been complimented and also with the shamed resolve that she would keep those pretty teeth white.

Tom's shoulders were becoming inclined to droop a little. To be sure, he was a little older than he used to be and sometimes very tired, but the droop was really caused more by carelessness than by anything else. When Jane came home from a visit to a friend whose husband was very round-shouldered indeed, she noticed more plainly than usual the beginning of the habit in Tom.

Choosing a moment when he straightened to his full height and squared his shoulders, she said: "Oh, Tom! I'm so glad you are tall and straight, not round-shouldered like Dick. He is growing worse every day until it is becoming a positive deformity with him." And Tom was glad she had not observed the tendency in his shoulders, and thereafter their straightness was noticeable.

Jane might have chosen a moment when Tom's shoulders were drooping and with perfect truthfulness have said:

"Tom! You are getting to be round-shouldered and ugly like Dick. In a little while you will look like a hunchback."

Tom would have felt hurt and resentful and probably would have retorted, "Well, you're getting older and uglier too," or something like that; and his hurt pride and vanity would have been a hindrance instead of a help to improvement.

The children, of course, get their bad tempers from their fathers, but I think we get our vanity from Adam, for we all have it, men and women alike; and like most things it is good when rightly used.

Tact may be trickery, but after all I think I prefer the dictionary definition—"nice discernment." To be tactful, one has only to discern or distinguish or, in other words, to see nicely and speak and act accordingly.

My sympathy just now, however, is very much with the persons who seem to be unable to say the right thing at the proper time. In spite of oneself there are times when one's mental fingers seem to be all thumbs. At a little gathering not long ago,

My sympathy just now, however, is very much with the persons who seem to be unable to say the right thing at the proper time.

I differed with the hostess on a question which arose and disagreed with just a shade more warmth than I intended.

35

I resolved to make it up by being a little extra sweet to her before I left.

The refreshments served were so dainty and delicious that I thought I would find some pleasant way to tell her so. But alas! As it was a very hot day, ice water was served after the little luncheon, and I found myself looking sweetly into my hostess's face and heard myself say, "Oh, wasn't that water good." What could one do after that, but murmur the conventional "Such a pleasant afternoon," at leaving and depart feeling like a little girl who had blundered at her first party.

Swearing
AUGUST 1918

I heard a boy swear the other day, and it gave me a distinctly different kind of shock than usual. I had just been reading an article in which our soldiers were called crusaders who were offering themselves in their youth as a sacrifice in order that right might prevail against wrong and that those ideals, which are, in effect, the teachings of Christ, shall be accepted as the law of nations.

When I heard the boy use the name of Christ in an oath, I felt that he had belittled the mighty effort we are making, and that he had put an affront upon our brave soldiers by using lightly the name of the great Leader who first taught the principles for which they are dying. The boy had not thought of it in this way at all. He imagined that he was being very bold and witty, quite a grown man in fact.

I wonder how things came to be so reversed from the right order that it should be thought daring and smart to swear instead of being regarded as utterly foolish and a sign of weakness, betraying a lack of self-control. If people could only realize how ridiculous they appear when they call down the wrath of the Creator and Ruler of the universe just because they have jammed their thumbs, I feel sure they would never be guilty of swearing again. It is so out of proportion, something as foolish and wasteful as it would be to use the long-range gun [a German artillery piece that could fire a shell seventy miles] which bombarded Paris to shoot a fly. If we call upon the Mightiest for trivial things, upon whom or what shall we call in the great moments of life?

> I wonder how things came to be so reversed ... that it should be thought daring and smart to swear instead of being regarded as ... a sign of weakness.

There are some things in the world which should be damned to the nethermost regions, but surely it is not some frightened animal whom our own lack of self-control has made rebellious or an inanimated object that our own carelessness has caused to smite us. Language loses its value when it is so misapplied, and in moments of real and great stress or danger we have nothing left to say.

It is almost hopeless to try to reform older persons who have the habit of swearing fastened upon them. Like any other habit, it is difficult to break, and it is useless to explain to them that it is a waste of force and nervous energy. But I think we should show children the absurdity of wasting the big shells of language on small insignificant objects.

Perhaps a little ridicule might prick that bubble of conceit, and the boy with his mouth full of his first oaths might not feel himself such a dashing daredevil of a fellow if he feared that he had made himself ridiculous.

Honor and Duty
OCTOBER 1919

Now can we depend on you in this?" asked Mr. Jones.

"Certainly you can," replied Mr. Brown. "I'll do it!"

"But you failed us before, you know," continued Mr. Jones, "and it made us a lot of trouble. How would it be for you to put up a forfeit? Will you put up some money as security that you will not fail; will you bet on it?"

"No-o-o," answered Mr. Brown. "I won't bet on it, but I'll give you my word of honor."

How much was Mr. Brown's word worth? I would not want to risk much on it. Would you? He evidently considered it of less value than a little cash. Now and then we hear of people whose word is as good as their bond, but far too often we find that "word of honor" is used carelessly and then forgotten or ignored.

> "It is so much easier to say 'yes,' and then do as I please afterward."

Speaking to a friend of the difficulties of putting through a plan we had in mind, I remarked that it was very difficult to do anything with a crowd any more, for so many would promise and then fail to keep the promise.

"I know," she replied, "I do that way myself; it is so much easier to say 'yes,' and then do as I please afterward."

If my friend had realized how weak and unkind her reason was for disregarding her word, she would be more careful, for she prides herself on her strength of character and is a very kind, lovable woman on the whole.

Mr. Brown and my friend had mistaken ideas of value. One's word is of infinitely more worth than money. If money is lost, more money, and just as good, is to be had; but if you pledge your word and do not redeem it, you have lost something that cannot be replaced. It is intangible perhaps but nevertheless valuable to you.

A person who cannot be depended upon by others, in time, becomes unable to depend upon himself. It seems in some subtle way to undermine and weaken the character when we do not hold ourselves strictly responsible for what we say.

And what a tangle it makes of all our undertakings when people do not keep their promises. How much pleasanter it would be, and how much more would be accomplished, if we did not give our word unless we intended to keep it, so that we would all know what we could depend upon!

When we think of honor we always think of duty in connection with it. They seem to be inseparably linked together. The following incident illustrates this.

> When we think of honor we always think of duty in connection with it.

Albert Bebe, a French resident of San Francisco, came home from the battlefront in France. He had been in the trenches for two years and four months in an advanced position, a "listening post" only sixty yards from the German trenches. Marie Bebe, the soldier's little daughter, was very much excited over her father's coming and objected to going to school the next morning. She thought she should be allowed to stay at home on the first day of her father's visit.

But her mother said: "No! Your father went to fight for France because it was his duty to go. You must go to school because that is your duty. Your father did his duty and you must do yours!" And Marie went to school.

If everybody did his duty as well in the smaller things, there would be no failures when the greater duties presented themselves.

Troubles Grow as We Talk about Them
JANUARY 1920

The snow was falling fast and a cold wind blowing the other morning. I had just come in from feeding the chickens and was warming my chilled self when the telephone rang.

"Hello!" said I, and a voice full of laughter came over a wire. "Good morning!" it said. "I suppose you are busy making garden today."

"Making garden?" I asked wonderingly.

> If we want vegetables, we must make them grow, not leave the ground barren where we have destroyed the weeds.

"Yes," replied the voice, "you said some time ago that you enjoyed making garden in the wintertime beside a good fire, so I thought you'd be busily at it this morning."

"Well," I replied defensively, "the vegetables one raises in the seed catalogs are so perfectly beautiful." And with a good laugh, we began the day right merrily in spite of the storm outside.

So after many days my words came back to me and the thoughts that followed them were altogether different from those connected with them before.

We do grow beautiful gardens beside the fire on cold winter days as we talk over the seed catalogs; and our summer gardens are much more of a success because of these gardens in our minds. We grow many other things in the same way. It is truly surprising how anything grows and grows by talking about it.

We have a slight headache and we mention the fact. As an excuse to ourselves for inflicting it upon our friends, we make it as bad as possible in the telling. "Oh, I have such a dreadful headache," we say and immediately we feel much worse. Our pain has grown by talking of it.

If there is a disagreement between friends and the neighbors begin talking about it, the difficulty grows like a jimsonweed, and the more it is talked about, the faster it grows.

When there is a disagreement between workmen and their employers, the agitators immediately begin their work of talking and the trouble grows and grows until strikes and lockouts and riots are ripened and harvested and the agitators grow fat on the fruits thereof.

The same law seems to work in both human nature and in the vegetable kingdom and in the world of ideas with the changes caused just by talk, either positive or negative. Even peas and cabbages grow by cultivation, by keeping the soil "stirred" about them.

Now, it isn't enough in any garden to cut down the weeds. The cutting out of weeds is important, but cultivating the garden plants is just as necessary. If we want vegetables, we must make them grow, not leave the ground barren where we have destroyed the weeds. Just so we must give much of our attention to the improvements we want, not all to the abuses we would like to correct. If we hope to improve conditions, any conditions, anywhere, we must do a great deal of talking about the better things.

If we have a headache we will forget it sooner if we talk of pleasant things. If there is misunderstanding and bad feeling between neighbors, we can cultivate their friend-liness by telling each of the other's kind words before the trouble began. Perhaps a crust has formed around the plant of their friendship, and it only needs that the soil should be stirred in order to keep on growing.

> Perhaps a crust has formed around the plant of their friendship, and it only needs that the soil should be stirred in order to keep on growing.

43

Keeping Friends
MARCH 1919

Sometimes we are a great trial to our friends and put an entirely uncalled-for strain upon our friendships by asking foolish questions.

The Man of the Place and I discovered the other day that we had for some time been saying to our friends, "Why don't you come over?" Can you think of a more awkward question than that? Just imagine the result if that question should always be answered truthfully. Some would reply, "Because I do not care to visit you." Others might say, "Because it is too much trouble," while still others who might care to come would be swamped in trying to enumerate the many little reasons why they had not done so. We decided that we would break ourselves of such a bad habit.

> The habit of saying disagreeable things or of being careless about how what we say affects others grows on us so easily and so surely if we indulge it.

I once had a neighbor who, whenever we met, invariably asked me why I had not been to visit her. Even when I did go she met me with the query, "Why haven't you been over before?" It was not a very pleasant greeting, and naturally one shuns unpleasantness when one may.

I have another neighbor who will call me on the phone and say: "It has been a long time since we have seen you, and we do want a good visit. Can't you come over tomorrow?" And immediately I wish to go. It does make such a difference how things are said.

Friendship is like love. It cannot be demanded or driven or insisted upon. It must be wooed to be won. The habit of saying disagreeable things or of being careless about how what we say affects others grows on us so easily and so surely if we indulge it.

"Mrs. Brown gave me an unhappy half hour a few days ago," said Mrs. Gray to me. "She said a great many unpleasant things and was generally disagreeable, but it is all right. The poor thing is getting childish, and we must overlook her oddities."

Mrs. Gray is a comparative newcomer in the neighborhood, but I have known Mrs. Brown for years; and ever since I have known her, she has prided herself on her plain speaking, showing very little regard for others' feelings. Her unkindness appears to me not a reversion to the mentality of childhood but simply an advance in the way she was going years ago. Her tongue has only become sharper with use, and her dexterity in hurting the feelings of others has grown with practice.

I know another woman of the same age whom no one

speaks of as being childish. It is not necessary to make such an excuse for her because she is still, as she has been for twenty years, helpful and sweet and kind. And this helpfulness and sweetness and kindness of hers has grown with the passing years. I think no one will ever say of her, "poor old thing, she is childish," as an excuse for her being disagreeable. I know she would hope to die before that time should come.

People do grow childish in extreme old age, of course, and should be treated with tenderness because of it; but I believe that even then the character which they have built during the years before will manifest itself. There is a great difference in children, you know, and I have come to the conclusion that if we live to reach a second childhood, we shall not be bad-tempered, disagreeable children unless we have indulged those traits.

> Friendship is like love. It cannot be demanded or driven or insisted upon. It must be wooed to be won.

Then there are the people who are "peculiar." Ever meet any of them?

The word seems to be less used than formerly, but there was a time when it was very common, and I longed to shriek every time I heard it.

"Oh! You must not do that; George will be angry. He is so peculiar!"

"Of course, she doesn't belong with the rest of the crowd, but I had to invite her. She is so peculiar, you know, and so easily offended."

"I wouldn't pay any attention to that. Of course, she did treat you abominably, but it is just her way. She is so peculiar."

And so on and on. I thought seriously of cultivating a reputation for being peculiar, for like charity such a reputation seemed to cover multitudes of sins; but I decided that it would be even more unpleasant for me than for the other fellow; that it would not pay to make myself an unlovely character for the sake of any little, mean advantage to be gained by it.

THREE

THE WINDOW THROUGH WHICH WE SEE THE WORLD

*"Things and persons appear to us according
to the light we throw upon them."*

Lesson from an Irish Fable
NOVEMBER 1922

Some time ago I read an Irish fairy story which told how a mortal, on a fairy steed, went hunting with the fairies. He had his choice of whether the fairy horse should become large enough to carry a man-sized man or be small enough to ride the horse as it was.

He chose to become of fairy size and, after the magic was worked, rode gaily with the fairy king until he came to a wall so high he feared his tiny

> "Throw your heart over the wall, then follow it!"

horse could not carry him over; but the fairy king said to him, "Throw your heart over the wall, then follow it!" So he rode fearlessly at the wall, with his heart already bravely past it, and went safely over.

I have forgotten most of the story and do not remember the name of the author, though I wish I did; but often I think of the fairy's advice. Anyone who has ridden horses much understands how the heart of the rider going over fairly lifts the horse up and across an obstacle. And I have been told, by good drivers, that it holds true in taking a motor car up a difficult hill.

But the uplift of a fearless heart will help us over other sorts of barriers. In any undertaking, to falter at a crisis means defeat. No one ever overcomes difficulties by going at them in a hesitant, doubtful way.

If we would win success in anything, when we come to a wall that bars our way, we must throw our hearts over and then follow confidently. It is fairy advice, you know, and savors of magic, so following it we will ride with the fairies of good fortune and go safely over.

The Armor of a Smile
NOVEMBER 1921

Mrs. A was angry. Her eyes snapped, her voice was shrill, and a red flag of rage was flying upon each cheek. She expected opposition and anger at the things she said, but her remarks were answered in a soft voice; her angry eyes were met by smiling ones; and her attack was smothered in the softness of courtesy, consideration, and compromise.

I feel sure Mrs. A had intended to create a disturbance, but she might as well have tried to break a feather pillow by beating it as to have any effect with her angry voice and manner on the perfect kindness and good manners which met her. She only made herself ridiculous, and in self-defense was obliged to change her attitude.

Since then I have been wondering if it always is so, if shafts of malice aimed in anger forever fall harmless against the armor of a smile, kind words, and gentle man-

> She might as well have tried to break a feather pillow by beating it.

ners. I believe they do. And I have gained a fuller understanding of the words, "A soft answer turneth away wrath."*

Until this incident, I had found no more in the words than the idea that a soft answer might cool the wrath of an aggressor, but I saw wrath turned away as an arrow deflected from its mark and came to understand that a soft answer and a courteous manner are an actual protection.

* Proverbs 15:1

Nothing is ever gained by allowing anger to have sway. While under its influence, we lose the ability to think clearly and lose the forceful power that is in calmness.

Anger is a destructive force; its purpose is to hurt and destroy, and being a blind passion, it does its evil work, not only upon whatever arouses it, but also upon the person who harbors it. Even physically it injures him, impeding the action of the heart and circulation, affecting the respiration, and creating an actual poison in the blood. Persons with weak hearts have been known to drop dead from it, and always there is a feeling of illness after indulging in a fit of temper.

Anger is a destroying force. What all the world needs is its opposite—an uplifting power.

Laura and Mary Quarrel at Thanksgiving
NOVEMBER 1916

As Thanksgiving Day draws near again, I am reminded of an occurrence of my childhood. To tell the truth, it is a yearly habit of mine to think of it about this time and to smile at it once more.

We were living on the frontier in South Dakota then. There's no more frontier within the boundaries of the United States, more's the pity, but then we were ahead of the railroad in a new unsettled country. Our nearest and only neighbor was twelve miles away, and the store was forty miles distant.

The home Pa Ingalls built for his family in De Smet

Father had laid in a supply of provisions for the winter, and among them were salt meats; but for fresh meat we depended on father's gun and the antelope which fed in herds across the prairie. So we were quite excited, one day near Thanksgiving, when Father hurried into the house for his gun and then away again to try for a shot at a belated flock of wild geese hurrying south.

We would have roast goose for Thanksgiving dinner! "Roast goose and dressing seasoned with sage," said sister Mary.

"No, not sage! I don't like sage, and we won't have it in the dressing," I exclaimed. Then we quarreled, sister Mary and I, she insisting that there should be sage in the dressing, and I declaring that there should not be sage in the dressing, until Father returned—without the goose!

I remember saying in a meek voice to sister Mary, "I wish I had let you have the sage," and to this day when I think of it, I feel again just as I felt then and realize how thankful I would have been for roast goose and dressing with sage seasoning—with or without any seasoning—I could even have gotten along without the dressing. Just plain goose roasted would have been plenty good enough.*

This little happening has helped me to be properly thankful even though at times the seasoning of my blessings has not been just such as I would have chosen.

"I suppose I should be thankful for what we have, but I can't feel very thankful when I have to pay $2.60 for a little flour and the price still going up," writes a friend, and in the same letter she says, "we are in our usual health." The family are so used to good health that it is not even taken into consideration as a cause of thanksgiving. We are so inclined to take for granted the blessings we possess

> I remember saying in a meek voice to sister Mary, "I wish I had let you have the sage."

---

* This story appears in chapter 26 of *By the Shores of Silver Lake*.

and to look for something peculiar, some special good luck for which to be thankful.

I read a Thanksgiving story the other day in which a woman sent her little boy out to walk around the block and look for something for which to be thankful.

One would think that the fact of his being able to walk around the block, and that he had a mother to send him, would have been sufficient cause for thankfulness. We are nearly all afflicted with mental farsightedness and so easily overlook the thing which is obvious and near. There are our hands

> Why, there is greater occasion for thankfulness just in the unimpaired possession of one of the five senses than there would be if someone left us a fortune.

and feet—who ever thinks of giving thanks for them, until indeed they, or the use of them, are lost?

We usually accept them as a matter of course, without a thought, but a year of being crippled has taught me the value of my feet and two perfectly good feet are now among my dearest possessions.* Why, there is

---

*Unfortunately, her husband, Almanzo, was somewhat crippled in both feet following a stroke early on in his marriage to Laura. He had become sick and had tried to get back to work too soon.

greater occasion for thankfulness just in the unimpaired possession of one of the five senses than there would be if someone left us a fortune. Indeed, how could the value of one be reckoned? When we have all five in good working condition, we surely need not make a search for anything else in order to feel that we should give thanks to Whom thanks are due.

I once remarked upon how happy and cheerful a new acquaintance seemed always to be, and the young man to whom I spoke replied, "Oh, he's just glad that he is alive." Upon inquiry, I learned that several years before, this man had been seriously ill; that there had been no hope of his living, but to everyone's surprise he had made a complete recovery, and since then he had always been remarkably happy and cheerful.

When the Blues Descend
AUGUST 1920

The whole world was a deep, dark blue, for I had waked with a grouch that morning. While blue is without doubt a heavenly color, it is better in skies than in one's mind; for when the blues descend upon a poor mortal on earth, life seems far from being worth the living.

I didn't want to help with the chores; I hated to get breakfast; and the prospect of doing up the morning's work afterward was positively revolting. Beginning the usual round of duties—under protest—I had a great many thoughts about work and none of them was complimentary to the habit. But presently my mind took a wider range and became less personal as applied to the day just beginning.

> "Six days shalt thou labour, and do all thy work."

First, I remembered the old, old labor law, "Six days shalt thou labour, and do all thy work: but the seventh day is the sabbath of the LORD thy God: in it thou shalt not do any work."*

It used to be impressed upon us as most important that we must rest on the seventh day. This doesn't seem to be necessary any longer. We may not "Remember the sabbath day, to keep it holy,"** but we'll not forget to stop working. With our present attitude toward work, the emphasis should be put upon, "Six days shalt thou labour," and if we stick it out to work the six days, we will rest on the seventh without any urging.

Given half a chance, we will take Saturday off also and any other day or part of a day we can manage to sneak, besides which the length of a workday is shrinking and

---

* Exodus 20:9–10
** Exodus 20:8

shrinking for everyone except farmers, and they are hoping to shorten theirs.

But really the old way was best, for it takes about six days of work to give just the right flavor to a day off. As I thought of all these things, insensibly, my ideas about work changed. I remembered the time of enforced idleness when recovering from an illness and how I longed to be busily at work again. Also I recollected a week of vacation that I once devoted to pleasure during which I suffered more than the weariness of working while I had none of its satisfaction. For there is a great satisfaction in work well done, the thrill of success in a task accomplished.

> There is nothing wrong with God's plan that man should earn his bread by the sweat of his brow. The wrong is in our own position only.

I got the thrill at the moment that my mind reached the climax. The separator was washed. It is a job that I especially dislike, but while my mind had been busy far afield, my hands had performed their accustomed task with none of the usual sense of unpleasantness, showing that, after all, it is not so much the work we do with our bodies that makes us tired and dissatisfied as the work we do with our minds.

We have been, for so long, thinking of labor as a curse

upon man that, because of our persistently thinking of it as such, it has very nearly become so.

There always has been a great deal of misplaced pity for Adam because of his sentence to hard labor for life when really that was all that saved him after he was deported from paradise, and it is the only thing that has kept his descendents as safe and sane even as they are.

There is nothing wrong with God's plan that man should earn his bread by the sweat of his brow. The wrong is in our own position only. In trying to shirk while we "let George do it," we bring upon ourselves our own punishment; for in the attitude we take toward our work, we make of it a burden instead of the blessing it might be.

Work is like other good things in that it should not be indulged in to excess, but a reasonable amount that is of value to one's self and to the world, as is any honest, well-directed labor, need never descend into drudgery.

It is a tonic and an inspiration and a reward unto itself. For the sweetness of life lies in usefulness like honey deep in the heart of a clover bloom.

The Creative Chemistry of Life
JULY 1921

It is hot in the kitchen these days cooking for the men in the hay harvest fields. But perhaps we are making ourselves more warm and tired than necessary by fretting and thinking how tired and warm we are. We would be much cooler and less tired if, instead of thinking of the weather and our weariness, we would try to remember the bird songs we heard in the early morning or notice the view of the woods and hills or of the valley and stream. It would help us to think of the cooling breeze on the porch where we rest in the evening's lengthening shadows when the long, hot day is over.

> There are pleasant things to think about and beauty to be found everywhere, and they grow by dwelling on them.

There are pleasant things to think about and beauty to be found everywhere, and they grow by dwelling on them. If we would but open our eyes to the beauty of our surroundings, we would be much happier and more comfortable. The kingdom of home, as well as the Kingdom of Heaven, is within us. It is pleasant and happy or the opposite according as our minds and hearts attune themselves to the beauty and joy around us or vibrate to thoughts of ugliness and discomfort.

Which leads me to conclude that our lives are like coal tar. This sounds rather unpleasant, but I'm sure I'll be pardoned for using the simile when it is clearly understood that I have no intention of blackening anyone's character. Coal tar is not altogether what it appears to be. A great many things can be taken from it. That's like life, isn't it—everybody's life?

Until recently I always thought of coal tar as a black, sticky, unpleasant substance, fit only for use as a roofing paint. But it is a wonderful combination of elements out of which may be made what one wills. The most beautiful colors, delightful perfumes, and delicious flavors are contained within its blackness and may be taken from it. It also contains valuable food elements and the most dreadful poisons. From it also are made munitions of war and the precious medicines that cure the wounds made by those same munitions.

And so our lives are similar in that we may make of them or get out of them what we choose—beauty and fragrance and usefulness or those things that are ugly and harmful. It is necessary to understand chemistry to extract from coal tar its valuable properties, and we must practice the "creative chemistry" of life to get true values from life.

Just as the chemist in his laboratory today is carrying on the work of the old-time alchemist, so we may practice magic arts. We may change unloveliness into beauty and, from the darkness of life, evolve all the beautiful colors of the rainbow of promise by developing the bright rays of purity and love, the golden glow of constancy, the true-blue of steadfastness, and the ever-green home of immortality.

The Light We Throw
FEBRUARY 1922

A wonderful way has been invented to transform a scene on the stage, completely changing the apparent surroundings of the actors and their costumes without moving an article. The change is made in an instant. By an arrangement of light and colors, the scenes are so painted that with a red light thrown upon them, certain parts come into view while other parts remain invisible. By changing a switch and throwing a blue light upon the scene, what has been visible disappears and things unseen before appear, completely changing the appearance of the stage.

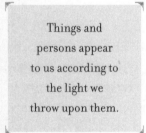

Things and persons appear to us according to the light we throw upon them.

This late achievement of science is a good illustration of a fact we all know but so easily forget or overlook— that things and persons appear to us according to the light we throw upon them from our own minds.

When we are downhearted and discouraged, we speak of looking at the world through blue glasses; nothing looks the same to us; our family and friends do not appear the same; our home and work show in the darkest colors. But when we are happy, we see things in a brighter light and everything is transformed.

How unconsciously we judge others by the light that is within ourselves, condemning or approving them by our own conception of right and wrong, honor and dishonor! We show by our judgment just what the light within us is.

What we see is always affected by the light in which we look at it so that no two persons see people and things alike. What we see and how we see depends upon the nature of our light.

A quotation, the origin of which I have forgotten, lingers in my mind: "You cannot believe in honor until you have achieved it. Better keep yourself clean and bright; you are the window through which you must see the world."

The Blessings of the Year
NOVEMBER 1922

Among all the blessings of the year, have you chosen one for which to be especially thankful at this Thanksgiving time, or are you unable to decide which is the greatest?

Sometimes we recognize as a special blessing what heretofore we have taken without a thought as a matter of course, as when we recover from a serious illness; just a breath drawn free from pain is a matter for rejoicing. If we have been crippled and then are whole again, the blessed privilege of walking forth free and unhindered seems a gift from the "gods." We must needs have been hungry to properly appreciate food, and we never love our friends as we should until they have been taken from us.

> We must needs have been hungry to properly appreciate food.

As the years pass, I am coming more and more to understand that it is the common, everyday blessings of our common, everyday lives for which we should be particularly grateful. They are the things that fill our lives with comfort and our hearts with gladness—just the pure air to breathe and the strength to breathe it; just warmth and shelter and home folks; just plain food that gives us strength; the bright sunshine on a cold day; and a cool breeze when the day is warm.

Oh, we have so much to be thankful for that we seldom think of it in that way! I wish we might think more about these things that we are so much inclined to overlook and live more in the spirit of the old Scotch table blessing.

Some hae meat wha canna' eat
And some can eat that lack it.
But I hae meat and I can eat
And sae the Laird be thankit. *

---

* From "The Selkirk Grace" by Robert Burns

FOUR

TO BE WELL-DEVELOPED
AND BALANCED

*"Lives . . . should be well-developed and
balanced, strong and symmetrical."*

An Autumn Day

King Winter has sent warning of his coming! There was a delightful freshness in the air the other morning, and all over the low places lay the first frost of the season.

What a beautiful world this is! Have you noticed the wonderful coloring of the sky at sunrise? For me there is no time like the early morning when the spirit of light broods over the earth at its awakening. What glorious colors in

> Why is the world so beautiful if not for us?

the woods these days! Did you ever think that great painters have spent their lives trying to reproduce on canvas what we may see every day? Thousands of dollars are paid for their pictures which are not so beautiful as those nature gives us freely. The colors in the sky at sunset, the delicate tints of the early spring foliage, the brilliant autumn leaves, the softly colored grasses and lovely flowers—what painter ever equaled their beauties with paint and brush?

I have in my living room three large windows uncovered by curtains which I call my pictures. Ever changing with the seasons, with wild birds and gay squirrels passing on and off the scene, I never have seen a landscape painting to compare with them.

As we go about our daily tasks, the work will seem lighter if we enjoy these beautiful things that are just outside our doors and windows. It pays to go to the top of the hill now and then to see the view and to stroll through the wood lot or pasture forgetting that we are in a hurry or that there is such a thing as a clock in the world. You are "so busy"! Oh, yes, I know it! We are all busy, but what are we living for anyway, and why is the world so beautiful if not for us? The habits we form last us through this life, and I firmly believe into the next. Let's not make such a habit of hurry and work that when we leave this world, we will feel impelled to hurry through the spaces of the universe using our wings for feather dusters to clean away the star dust.

The true way to live is to enjoy every moment as it passes, and surely it is in the everyday things around us that the beauty of life lies.

> I strolled today down a woodland path—
> A crow cawed loudly and flew away.
> The sky was blue and the clouds were gold
> And drifted before me fold on fold;
> The leaves were yellow and red and brown
> And patter, patter the nuts fell down,
> On this beautiful, golden autumn day.
>
> A squirrel was storing his winter hoard,
> The world was pleasant: I lingered long,
> The brown quails rose with a sudden whirr
> And a little bundle, of eyes and fur,
> Took shape of a rabbit and leaped away.
> A little chipmunk came out to play
> And the autumn breeze sang a wonder song.

Simplify, Simplify
JULY 1919

Rummaging through a closet in the attic a few days ago, I unearthed some fashion magazines of the summer of 1908 and was astonished to discover that since that short time ago women have apparently changed the form of their bodies and the shape of their faces as well as the style of their gowns and hair dressing.

Perhaps the pensive lines and die-away expression of the faces in the old-fashioned plates were due to the tightly drawn-in waists and the over-drawn-check effect of the choker collars, or it may be that faces with such an expression just naturally called for that style of dressing.

> The world is full of so many things, so many of them useless . . . It would be a wonderful relief if, by eliminating both wisely and well, life might be simplified.

However that may be, a comparison of those fashions with the easy, comfortable styles of this summer, which give beauty and grace of line with freedom of movement and plenty of breathing room, is enough cause for celebrating a special Thanksgiving Day months ahead of the regular time.

There is still room for improvement in children's clothes. They are much too fussy to be either beautiful or becoming. Why trouble with fancy, changeable children's styles? There will be plenty of time for them to learn all the vanities of dress later, and it is better to keep them simple and sweet as long as possible. It would do away with a lot of needless bother and vexation if we copied the English in their way of dressing little girls as their mothers were dressed, in the same kind of a simple little smock frock.

Fashions in other things than clothes have been and are still being simplified for the sake of a more economic production, thus lessening the cost of manufacturing by saving time, labor, and material.

Furniture makers cut down the number of their patterns several hundred percent during the war, cutting out just that many varieties of furniture. This was done on the advice of the War Industries Board to reduce the cost of production and save materials and labor for other work. It was found to be such a benefit that it has been decided to keep on in the same way, and so we shall have fewer styles in furniture.

> Fashions in other things than clothes have been and are still being simplified for the sake of a more economic production.

In the hardware trade the same plan is being used. There are something like 4,450 fewer styles of pocket knives for Johnnie to buy and lose than there were before the war, but it does seem that he should be able to please himself by a choice from the 250 kinds left him.

There used to be 207 kinds of lawnmowers. Now there are only 6. This number does not include the regular mowing machine which the Man of the Place uses so effectively in the front yard nor the pet colt who mows the lawn and puts the clippings to such good use.

The idea of doing away with useless, unnecessary things is at work in architecture also in the planning and building of houses, so that we are hearing a great deal these days of the dining-roomless house.

The dining room, if kept strictly as a dining room, is used for only a few minutes three times a day, which is not enough return for the work and thought and expense of keeping up an extra room. The fact is that most dining rooms are used by the family as a living room as well, and so in the new plans, the rooms are frankly combined into one.

Sometimes where the kitchen is large, it is the kitchen and dining room and many steps are saved. Either of these combination rooms may be made very attractive and have been in small houses where people did not wait for it to become the fashion.

Everyone is complaining of being tired, of not having time for what they wish to do. It is no wonder when they are obliged to pick and choose from such multitudes of thoughts and things.

The world is full of so many things, so many of them useless, so many, many varieties of the same thing creating confusion and a feeling of being overwhelmed by their number. It would be a wonderful relief if, by eliminating both wisely and well, life might be simplified.

Compensations
NOVEMBER 1919

One gains a lot by going out into the world, by traveling and living in different places," Rose said to me one day, "but one loses a great deal, too. After all, I'm not sure but the loss is greater than the gain."

"Just how do you mean?" I asked. "I mean this," said Rose. "The best anyone can get out of this world is happiness and contentment, and people here in the country

Herbert Hoover Presidential Library

Rose, Laura's progressive-thinking daughter

seem so happy and contented, so different from the restless people of the cities who are out in the rush of things."

So after all, there are compensations. Though we do not have the advantages of travel, we stay-at-homes may acquire a culture of the heart that is almost impossible in the rush and roar of cities.

> A friend writes me of New York, "I like it and I hate it."

I think there are always compensations. The trouble is we do not recognize them. We usually are so busily longing for things we can't have that we overlook what we have in their place that are even more worthwhile. Sometimes we realize our happiness only by comparison after we have lost it. It really appears to be true that

To appreciate heaven well

A man must have some fifteen minutes of hell.

Talking with another friend from the city gave me still more of an understanding of this difference between country and city.

"My friends in town always are going somewhere. They never are quiet a minute if they can help it," he said. "Always they are looking for something to pass the time away quickly as though they were afraid to be left by themselves. The other evening one of the fellows was all broken up because there was nothing doing. There isn't a thing on for tonight, he said. Not a thing! He seemed to think it was something terrible that there was nothing special on hand for excitement, and he couldn't bear to think of spending a quiet evening at home."

What an uncomfortable condition to be in—depending altogether on things outside of one's self for happiness and a false happiness at that, for the true must come from within.

If we are such bad company that we can't live with ourselves, something is seriously wrong and should be attended to, for sooner or later we shall have to face ourselves alone.

There seems to be a madness in the cities, a frenzy in the struggling crowds. A friend writes me of New York, "I like it and I hate it. There's something you've got to love, it's so big—a people hurrying everywhere, all trying to live and be someone or something—and then, when you see the poverty and hatefulness, the uselessness of it all, you wonder why people live here at all. It does not seem possible that there are any peaceful farms on the earth."

> I am thankful for the peacefulness and comparative isolation of country life.

And so more than ever I am thankful for the peacefulness and comparative isolation of country life. This is a happiness which we ought to realize and enjoy.

We who live in the quiet places have the opportunity to become acquainted with ourselves, to think our own thoughts, and live our own lives in a way that is not possible for those who are keeping up with the crowd, where there is always something "on for tonight," and who have become so accustomed to crowds that they are dependent upon them for comfort.

> *In thine own cheerful spirit live,*
> *Nor seek the calm that others give;*
> *For thou, thyself, alone must stand*
> *Not held upright by other's hand.*

To Stand by Ourselves
APRIL 1920

Out in the woods the other day, I saw a tree that had branches on only one side. Evidently, other trees had grown so near it that there had been room for it to grow in only the one way, and now that it was left to stand alone its lack of good development and balance showed plainly.

It was not a beautiful thing. It looked lopsided and freakish and unable to stand by itself, being pulled a little over by the weight of its branches. It reminded me of a person who has grown all in one direction; in his work perhaps, knowing how to do only one thing as those workmen in factories who do a certain thing to one part of a machine day after day and never learn how to complete the whole, depending on others to finish the job.

Or a woman who is interested in nothing but her house-work and gossip, leaving her life bare of all the beautiful branches of learning and culture which might have been hers.

Or that person who follows always the same habits of thought, thinking always along the same lines in the same safe, worn grooves, distrusting the new ideas that begin to branch out in other directions leading into new fields of thought where free winds blow.

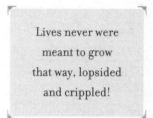

Lives never were meant to grow that way, lopsided and crippled!

And so many are dwarfed and crooked because of their ignorance on all subjects except a very few with the branches of their tree of knowledge all on one side!

Lives never were meant to grow that way, lopsided and crippled! They should be well-developed and balanced, strong and symmetrical, like a tree that grows by itself against the storms from whatever direction they may come—a thing of beauty and satisfaction.

The choice lies with us as to which we shall resemble. We may be like the young woman devoted to dress and fancywork who, when asked to join a club for the study of current events, replied, "What! Spend all the afternoon studying and talking about such things as that! Well, I should say not!"

Or, if we prefer, we may be like Mr. and Mrs. A. Mr. A is a good farmer; his crops and livestock are of the best, and besides he is a leader in farm organizations. Mrs. A is a good housekeeper; her garden is the best in the neighborhood, and her poultry is the pride of her heart.

As you see, they are very busy people, but they keep informed on current affairs and, now that the son and daughter are taking charge of part of the farm work, are having more time for reading and study. Their lives are branching out more and more in every direction for good to themselves and other people, for it is a fact that the more we make of our lives the better it is for others as well as ourselves.

You must not understand me to mean that we should selfishly live to ourselves. We are all better for contact and companionship with other people. We need such contact to polish off the rough corners of our minds and our manners, but it is a pitiful thing when anyone cannot, if necessary, stand by himself sufficient to himself and in good company even though alone.

The Things That Matter
JANUARY 1924

Standing on the shore with the waves of the Pacific rolling to my feet, I looked over the waters as far as my eyes could reach until the gray of the ocean merged with the gray of the horizon's rim. One could not be distinguished from the other. Where, within my vision, the waters stopped and the skies began I could not tell, so softly they blended one into the other. The waves rolled in regularly, beating a rhythm of time, but the skies above them were unmeasured—so vast and far-reaching that the mind of man could not comprehend it.

A symbol of time and of eternity—time spaced by our counting into years, breaking at our feet as the waves break on the shore; and eternity, unmeasurable as the skies above us—blending one into the other at the farthest reach of our earthly vision.

> We are so overwhelmed with things these days that our lives are all more or less cluttered.

As the New Year comes, seemingly with ever-increasing swiftness, there is a feeling that life is too short to accomplish the things we must do. But there is all eternity blending with the end of time for the things that really are worthwhile.

We are so overwhelmed with things these days that our lives are all, more or less, cluttered. I believe it is this, rather than a shortness of time, that gives us that feeling of hurry and almost of helplessness. Everyone is hurrying and usually just a little late. Notice the faces of the people who rush past on the streets or on our country roads! They nearly all have a strained, harassed look, and anyone you meet will tell you there is no time for anything anymore.

Life is so complicated! The day of the woman whose only needed tool was a hairpin is long since passed. But we might learn something from her and her methods even yet, for life would be pleasanter with some of the strain removed—if it were no longer true, as someone has said, that "things are in the saddle and rule mankind."

Here is a good New Year's resolution for us all to make: To simplify our lives as much as possible, to overcome that feeling of haste by remembering that there are just as many hours in the day as ever, and that there is time enough for the things that matter if time is rightly used.

Then, having done the most we may here, when we reach the limit of time, we will sail on over the horizon rim to new beauties and greater understanding.

We Keep Right on Eating
JANUARY 1922

With the holidays safely past, it is a good time to make resolutions not to overeat. It is easy to do so just after eating too much of too many good things.

We do eat too much! Everyone says so! But we keep

right on eating. I remember a neighborhood dinner I attended recently. You who have been to such dinners know how the table was loaded. There were breads and meats; vegetables and salads; pies of every kind, with flakey crusts and sweet, juicy fillings; cakes—loaf, layer, cup, white, yellow, pink, chocolate, iced, and plain; pickles, preserves, and canned fruit and such quantities of it all! We ate all we could and then some.

Then I learned of a dinner prepared for guests in the mountains of Albania* to which the neighbors were bidden. The food was coarse cornbread made without leavening, sweet and nutty, and so precious that the tiniest crumb, if dropped on the floor or table, must be picked up, kissed, and the sign of the cross made over it. Lean pork, stripped of every scrap of fat, was broiled on sticks over the fire.

> We ate all we could and then some.

In Albania it is etiquette to leave a great deal of the food, and it was sent away while the guests were still hungry. Then a wooden bowl filled with cubes of fat pork fried crisp was brought. This was also removed before hunger was satisfied, and water was brought for washing the

---

*Her daughter, Rose Wilder Lane, wrote of Albania in *The Peaks of Shala.*

hands. The strangers who were guests ate first, then the neighbors ate, and, after them, the family who entertained.

"In Albania it is not good manners to show eagerness for food," said the guide. "Albanians are not greedy."

The Hidden Cost of Getting What We Want
APRIL 1917

We were speaking of a woman in the community who was ignoring the conventions, thereby bringing joy to the gossips' hearts and a shock to those persons who always think first of what people will say.

"Well, of course," said my friend, "it is all perfectly harmless, and she has the satisfaction of doing as she pleases; but I'm wondering whether it's worth the price."

> Is there something in life that you want very much? Then pay the price and take it, but never expect to . . . avoid paying the bills.

There are very few things in this world that we may not have if we are willing to pay their price. You know, it has been said that "Every man has his price," which may or may not be true; but without doubt nearly every other thing has its market value, and we may make our choice and buy. We must pay, in one way or another, a greater or less amount for everything we have, and sometimes we show very poor judgment in our purchases.

Many a woman and girl has paid her good eyesight for a few pieces of hand embroidery or her peace of mind for a new gown, while many a man's good health or good standing in the community goes to pay for his indulgence in a bad habit.

Is there something in life that you want very much? Then pay the price and take it, but never expect to have a charge account and avoid paying the bills. Life is a good collector and sooner or later the account must be paid in full. I know a woman who is paying a debt of this kind on the installment plan. She wanted to be a musician and so she turned her children into the streets and neglected her husband that she might have more time for practice. She already has paid too high a price for her musical education, and the worst of it is that she will keep on paying the installments for the rest of her life.

> We buy many things we do not need, nor want, nor know just what to do with, and we pay for them much more than they are worth.

There are persons who act as if the things life has to offer were on sale at an auction, and if someone else is likely to secure an article, they will raise their bid without regard to the value of the goods on sale. Indeed, most of us are like people at an auction in this respect, that during the excitement and rivalry, we buy many things we do not need, nor want, nor know just what to do with, and we pay for them much more than they are worth.

Is it your ambition to outshine your neighbors and friends? Then you are the foolish bidder at the auction, raising your bid just because someone else is bidding. I knew a man like this. He owned a motor car of the same size and make as those of his friends but decided he would buy a larger, more powerful, and much more expensive one. His old car was good enough for all his needs, he said, but he was going to have a car that would be "better than the other fellows."

I suppose he figured the cost of the car in dollars and cents, but the real price he paid was in his integrity and business honor, and, for a bonus, an old and valued friendship. He had very poor judgment as a buyer, in my opinion.

Do you desire an education? No matter who pays the money for this, you cannot have it unless you also pay with long hours of study and application.

Do you wish to be popular? Then there is a chance to buy the real, lasting thing, which means to be well thought of and beloved by people worthwhile, or [to have] the shoddy imitation, a cheap popularity of the "hail fellow well met" sort depending mostly on one's ability to tell a good story and the amount one is able to spend on so-called pleasure. As always, the best is the cheapest, for poor goods are dear at any price: the square dealing, the kindness and consideration for others, the helpfulness and love, which we must spend if we wish lasting esteem to enrich us in the paying besides, bringing us what we so much desired.

There is a chance to buy the real, lasting thing, which means to be well thought of and beloved by people.

On the other hand, in buying a cheap popularity, people sometimes bankrupt themselves in things the value of which cannot be estimated. If popular favor must be paid for by the surrender of principles or loss of character, then indeed the price is too high.

FIVE

MAKE YOUR DREAM
A REALITY

"The dream is only the beginning."

Make Your Garden!

FEBRUARY 1918

Now is the time to make garden! Anyone can be a successful gardener at this time of year, and I know of no pleasanter occupation these cold, snowy days than to sit warm and snug by the fire, making garden with a pencil— in a seed catalog. What perfect vegetables we do raise in that way and so many of them! Our radishes are crisp and sweet, our lettuce tender, and our tomatoes smooth and beautifully colored. Best of all, there is not a bug or worm in the whole garden, and the work is so easily done.

In imagination we see the plants in our spring garden,

all in straight, thrifty rows with the fruits of each plant and vine numerous and beautiful as the pictures before us. How near the real garden of next summer approaches the ideal garden of our winter fancies depends upon how practically we dream and how we work.

It is so much easier to plan than it is to accomplish. When I started my small flock of Leghorns a few years ago, a friend inquired as to the profits of the flock and, taking my accounts as a basis, he figured I would be a millionaire within five years. The five years are past, but, alas, I am still obliged to be economical. There was nothing wrong with my friend's figuring except that he left out the word *if*, and that made all the difference between profits figured out on paper and those worked out by actual experience.

> He figured
> I would be a
> millionaire
> within five years.

My Leghorns would have made me a millionaire—if the hens had performed according to schedule; if the hawks had loved field mice better than spring chickens; if I had been so constituted that I never became weary; if prices—but why enumerate? Because allowance for that word *if* was not made in the figuring, the whole result was wrong.

It is necessary that we dream now and then. No one ever achieved anything from the smallest object to the greatest unless the dream was dreamed first. Those who stop at dreaming never accomplish anything.

We must first see the vision in order to realize it; we must have the ideal or we cannot approach it; but when once the dream is dreamed, it is time to wake up and "get busy." We must "do great deeds, not dream them all day long."

The dream is only the beginning. We'd starve to death if we went no further with that garden than making it by the fire in the seed catalog. It takes judgment to plant the seeds at the right time, in the right place, and hard digging to make them grow, whether in the vegetable garden or in the garden of our lives.

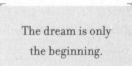

The dream is only the beginning.

We can work our dreams out into realities if we try, but we must be willing to make the effort. Things that seem easy of accomplishment in dreams require a lot of good common sense to put on a working basis and a great deal of energy to put through to a successful end. When we make our dream gardens, we must take into account the hot sun and the blisters on our hands; we must make allowance for and guard against the "ifs" so that when the time to work has come, they will not be of so much importance.

We may dream those dreams of our own, of a comfortable home, of that education we are going to have and those still more excellent dreams of the brotherhood of man and liberty and justice for all; then let us work to make this "the land where dreams come true."

Opportunity
NOVEMBER 1918

Grasp opportunity by the forelock, for it is bald behind," says the old proverb. In other words, we must be ready to meet and take advantage of opportunities as they come, or we will lose the chance. We cannot have any hold on them once they have passed by. Nor is time and endeavor spent in preparing ourselves ever wasted, for if we are ready, opportunity is sure to come.

No one can become great who is not ready to take the opportunity when it comes, nor indeed succeed in smaller matters; and whatever we prepare ourselves to do or become, the opportunity will come to us to do or become that thing.

Even though we never become one of the great persons of the world, the chance is sure to come to us to use whatever knowledge we acquire.

I knew a woman who denied herself in other things in

order that she might pay for French lessons. There seemed no chance that it would ever be an advantage to her except as a means of culture, but she now has a good position at a large salary which she would have been unable to fill but for her knowledge of French.

> Even though we never become one of the great persons of the world, the chance is sure to come to us to use whatever knowledge we acquire.

There is unfortunately a reverse side to this picture I have drawn of efforts crowned by success. Just as achievements are made possible by a careful preparation, a lack of effort to reach forward and beyond our present position works inversely, and again examples are too numerous to mention.

A hired man on a farm who always needs a boss, who is unable mentally and by disposition to work unless his employer is present and leading, who never fits himself by being responsible and trustworthy for the responsibility of owning and running his own farm, will always be a hired man either on a farm or elsewhere.

The tenant farmer who is not preparing himself for being an owner by putting himself mentally in an owner's place, getting his point of view and realizing his difficulties, is the tenant farmer who is always having trouble with his landlord and almost never comes to own his own farm. Realizing the difficulties and solving the problems of the next step up seem to lead inevitably to taking that step.

If we do a little less than is required by the position we now fill, whether in our own business or working for someone else; if we do not learn something of the work of the person higher up, we are never ready to advance, and then we say, "I had a good chance if I had only known how," and so forth.

No one can become great who is not ready to take the opportunity when it comes . . .

If we spend on our living every cent of our present income, we are not ready to take that opportunity which requires a little capital, and then we say, "That was a good chance if I could only have raised the money."

There is also a touch of humor to be found in the fact that what we prepare for comes to us, although it is rather pitiful. Humor and pathos are very close "kin."

When the influenza came to our town, Mrs. C called a friend and tried to engage her to come and nurse her through the illness.

"Have you the influenza?" asked the friend.

"Oh, no!" replied Mrs. C. "None of us has it yet, but I'm all ready for it. I have my bed all clean and ready to crawl into as soon as I feel ill. Everything is ready but a nurse, and I want you to come and take care of me."

In very few days, Mrs. C was in bed with an attack of influenza. She had prepared for the visit, and she could say with the psalmist: "The thing that I feared has come upon me" [Close! Actually, the quote is from Job chapter 3, verse 25].

Make Every Minute Count
MARCH 1918

Spring has come! The wild birds have been singing the glad tidings for several days, but they are such optimistic little souls that I always take their songs of spring with a grain of pessimism. The squirrels and chipmunks have been chattering to me, telling the same news, but they are such cheerful busybodies that I never believe quite all they say.

> I knew then that spring was here, for the sign of the picnickers is more sure than that of singing birds.

But now I know that spring is here, for as I passed the little creek on my way to the mailbox this morning, I saw scattered papers caught on the bushes, empty cracker and sandwich cartons strewn

99

around on the green grass, and discolored pasteboard boxes soaking in the clear water of the spring.

I knew then that spring was here, for the sign of the picnickers is more sure than that of singing birds and tender green grass, and there is nothing more unlovely than one of nature's beauty spots defiled in this way. It is such an unprovoked offense to nature, something like insulting one's host after enjoying his hospitality. It takes just a moment to put back into the basket the empty boxes and paper, and one can depart gracefully leaving the place all clean and beautiful for the next time or the next party.

Did you ever arrive all clean and fresh, on a beautiful summer morning, at a pretty picnic place and find that someone had been before you, and that the place was all littered up with dirty papers and buzzing flies? If you have and have ever left a place in the same condition, it served you right. Let's keep the open spaces clean, not fill them up with rubbish!

~

It is so easy to get things cluttered up—one's days, for instance, as well as picnic places—to fill them with empty, useless things and so make them unlovely and tiresome. Even though the things with which we fill our days were once important, if they are serving no good purpose now, they have become trash like the empty boxes and papers of the picnickers. It will pay to clean this trash away and keep our days as uncluttered as possible.

There are just now so many things that must be done that we are tempted to spend ourselves recklessly, especially as it is rather difficult to decide what to eliminate; and we cannot possibly accomplish everything. We must continually be weighing and judging and discarding things that are presented to us if we would save ourselves and spend our time and strength only on those things that are important. We may be called upon to spend our health and strength to the last bit, but we should see to it that we do not waste them.

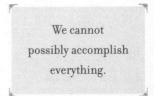

We cannot possibly accomplish everything.

"Oh, I am so tired that I just want to sit down and cry," a friend confided to me, "and here is the club meeting on hand and the lodge practice and the Red Cross workday and the aid society meeting and the church bazaar to get ready for, to say nothing of the pie supper at the schoolhouse and the spring sewing and garden and—Oh! I don't see how I'm ever going to get through it all!"

Of course, she was a little hysterical. It didn't all have to be done at once, but it showed how overtired she was, and it was plain that something must give way—if nothing else, herself. My friend needed a little open space in her life.

We must none of us shirk. We must do our part in every way, but let's be sure we clear away the rubbish, that we do nothing for empty form's sake nor because someone else does, unless it is the thing that should be done.

Challenges
AUGUST 1918

A difficulty raiseth the spirit of a great man. He hath a mind to wrestle with it and give it a fall. A man's mind must be very low if the difficulty doth not make part of his pleasure." By the test of these words of Lord Halifax, there are a number of great persons in the world today.

> Yes! And find pleasure in the difficulty for the sheer joy of surmounting it.

After all, what is a difficulty but a direct challenge? "Here I am in your way," it says, "you cannot get around me nor overcome me! I have blocked your path!" Anyone of spirit will accept the challenge and find some way to get around or over or through that obstacle. Yes! And find pleasure in the difficulty for the sheer joy of surmounting it as well as because there has been an opportunity once more to prove one's strength and cunning and, by the very use of these qualities, cause an increase of them.

The overcoming of one difficulty makes easier the conquering of the next until finally we are almost invincible. Success actually becomes a habit through the determined overcoming of obstacles as we meet them one by one.

If we are not being successful, if we are more or less on the road toward failure, a change in our fortunes can be brought by making a start, however small, in the right direction and then following it up. We can form the habit of success by beginning with some project and putting it through to a successful conclusion, however long and hard we must fight to do so, by "wrestling with" one difficulty and "giving it a fall." The next time it will be easier.

For some reason, of course, according to some universal law, we gather momentum as we proceed in whatever way we go; and just as by overcoming a small difficulty, we are more able to conquer the next, though greater; so if we allow ourselves to fail, it is easier to fail the next time, and failure becomes a habit until we are unable to look a difficulty fairly in the face, but turn and run from it.

There is no elation equal to the rise of the spirit to meet and overcome a difficulty, not with a foolish overconfidence but by keeping things in their proper relations by praying, now and then, the prayer of a good fighter whom I used to know: "LORD, make me sufficient to mine own occasion."

Make a New Beginning
JANUARY 1918

We should bring ourselves to an accounting at the beginning of the New Year and ask these questions: What have I accomplished? Where have I fallen short of what I desired and planned to do and be?

> I never have been in favor of making good resolutions on New Year's Day just because it was the first day of the year.

I never have been in favor of making good resolutions on New Year's Day just because it was the first day of the year. Any day may begin a new year for us in that way, but it does help some to have a set time to go over the year's efforts and see whether we are advancing or falling back.

If we find that we are quicker of temper and sharper of tongue than we were a year ago, we are on the wrong road. If we have less sympathy and understanding for others and are more selfish than we used to be, it is time to take a new path.

I helped a farmer figure out the value of his crops raised during the last season recently, and he was a very astonished person. Then when we added to that figure the amount he had received for livestock during the same period, he said: "It doesn't seem as if a man who had taken in that much off his farm would need a loan."

This farmer friend had not kept any accounts and so was surprised at the money he had taken in and that it should all be spent. Besides the help in a business way, there are a great many interesting things that can be gotten out of farm accounts if they are rightly kept.

The Man of the Place and I usually find out something new and unexpected when we figure up the business at the end of the year. We discovered this year that the two of us, without any outside help, had produced enough in the last year to feed thirty persons for a year—all the bread, butter, meat, eggs, sweetening, and vegetables necessary— and this does not include the beef cattle sold off the place.

So if you have not done so, just figure up for yourselves, and you will be surprised at how much you have accomplished.

The Source of Improvement
FEBRUARY 1917

I cannot stand still in my work. If I do not keep studying and going ahead, I slip back," said a friend the other day.

"Well, neither can I in my work," I thought. My mind kept dwelling on the idea. Was there a work that one could learn to do with a certain degree of excellence, and then keep that perfection without a ceaseless effort to advance?

Laura's writing desk

How easy and delightful life might be if we could do this, if when we had attained the position we wished, we might rest on our oars and watch the ripples on the stream of life.

Turning my mind resolutely from the picture of what would happen to the person who rested on his oars, expecting to hold his position where the tide was rippling, I began looking around for that place in life where one could stand still, without troubling to advance and without losing what already had been gained.

> Our friends and neighbors are either better friends and neighbors today than they were several years ago or they are not so good.

My friend who plays the piano so beautifully was a fair performer years ago but has improved greatly as time has gone by. She spends several hours every day at the instrument practicing. "I have to practice," she says, "or I shall lose my power of execution," and because she does practice to keep what she already has, she goes on improving from day to day and from year to year.

In contrast to this is the other friend who used to sing so much and who had such a lovely voice. She hardly ever sings now and told me the other day that she thought she was losing her voice. She also said that she was so busy, she had no time to practice.

There is also the woman who "completed her education" some years ago. She thought there was no need for further effort along that line and that she had her education for all time, so she settled down to the housework and the poultry. She had read very little of anything that would help her to keep abreast of the times and does not now give the impression of being an educated, cultured person, but quite the reverse. No doubt she has forgotten more than I ever knew, but the point is that she has lost it. Refusing to go ahead, she has dropped back.

Even a housekeeper who is a good housekeeper and stays such becomes a better and more capable one from the practice and exercise of her art and profession. If she does not, you may be sure she is slipping back, and instead of being proficient will soon be careless, a woman who will say, "I used to be a good housekeeper, but—"

The same rule applies to character. Our friends and neighbors are either better friends and neighbors today than they were several years ago or they are not so good. We are either broader minded, more tolerant and sympathetic now than we used to be, or the reverse is true. The person who is selfish or mean or miserly—does he not grow more so as the years pass, unless he makes a special effort to go in the other direction?

Our graces are either growing or shrinking. It seems to be a law of nature that everything and every person must move along. There is no standing still. The moment that growth stops, decay sets in.

One of the greatest safeguards against becoming old is that of continuing to grow mentally, you know.

If we do not strive to gain, we lose what we already have, for just so surely as "practice makes perfect," the want of practice or the lack of exercise of talents and knowledge makes for the opposite condition.

> It seems to be a law of nature that everything and every person must move along.

We must advance or we slip back, and few of us are bright enough to turn a slip to good account as did the school boy of long ago. This particular boy was late at school one icy winter morning, and the teacher reproved him and asked the reason for his tardiness.

"I started early enough," answered Tom, "but it was so slippery that every time I took one step ahead I slipped back two steps."

There was a hush of astonishment, and then the teacher asked, "But if that is true, how did you ever get here?"

"Oh, that's easy," replied Tom. "I was afraid I was going to be late and so I just turned around and came backwards."

Learning Something New
APRIL 1924

The topic that had been given me for my club lesson was music. Now, the only instrument I can play is the phonograph, and I venture to sing only in a crowd where I can drown my voice in the volume of sound. To be sure, I have a little music in my feet, but that would not answer for a club paper, so it seemed rather hopeless; but never yet have I been "stumped." I began to dig up just plain facts about music and seldom have I found anything so interesting.

The simple fact of how music came to have written form takes us away into the days of chivalry in the sixteenth century. To guide the choir boys in following the melody when singing masses, the monks wrote the Latin words, not in a straight line but up and down, to indicate their place in the musical scale. Later, to shorten the time and labor of writing, the words were replaced by circles, and the horizontal lines of the staff were added to more clearly indicate their position. Slowly, from time to time, the different forms of notes were made and music was

> I began to dig up just plain facts about music and seldom have I found anything so interesting.

standardized into the base and treble clefs so that our music of today takes its printed form directly from the manuscripts so laboriously written by hand in the monasteries of the sixteenth century.

This is only one of the many things I learned about music, but I learned also that it isn't what one already knows that adds interest to the preparation of a club paper so much as the learning something new in order to be able to go on with it.

Learning things is most fascinating, and I think it adds joy to life to be continually learning things so that we may be able to go on with it creditably.

ABOUT THE AUTHOR

Laura Ingalls Wilder (1867–1957) began writing, at age sixty-five, a series of eight children's books about her life in the pioneer West. These books were later turned into a world-renowned TV series. We all came to know and love Laura and her family either through the TV series or through the books. Yet twenty years before she even started the series, Wilder wrote articles for regional newspapers and magazines. *Writings to Young Women* is a collection of these articles.

ABOUT THE EDITOR

Stephen W. Hines has loved Laura Ingalls Wilder's books since he was a boy, and this love is evident in the careful research and arrangement of these delightful articles. Hines graduated from the University of Kansas and received his MA in journalism from Ball State University in Muncie, Indiana. He has worked in publishing since 1979. More than six hundred thousand of his books are currently in print.